The Preschool Church

Church School Lessons
For Three- To Five-Year-Olds

Eve Parker

CSS Publishing Company, Inc., Lima, Ohio

Copyright © 1996 by
CSS Publishing Company, Inc.
Lima, Ohio

Library of Congress Cataloging-in-Publication Data

Parker, Eve, 1960-
    The preschool church : church school lessons for three to five year olds / Eve Parker.
        p.   cm.
    ISBN 0-7880-0848-X
    1. Christian education of preschool children. I. Title.
BV1475.8.P37   1996
268'.432—dc20   96-6866
                                                                          CIP

ISBN 0-7880-0848-X
PRINTED IN U.S.A.

To the children of First Church,
who are always challenging,
enlightening, and lovable.

Table Of Contents

Chapter One

You're A Teacher!

The Importance Of Beginning

My first memories of church are preschool Church School classes. I treasure a photograph of my class, our Sunday best clothes askew from playing.

I suspect the same is true for most people raised in the church.

The preschool class is important. It is the beginning of a child's relationship with her church, separate from her parents. The strength of this relationship, nurtured over the years to come, will determine whether she remains faithful.

Church friendships begin in preschool, four and five year olds with growing social skills learning each others names and playing together. These little children eventually become the teenagers we want to attend youth group. How much more likely they are to enjoy youth group if they are meeting old playmates.

A child's connection to Christ begins at this time as well. Preschoolers are full of questions about life and people and nature. They are fascinated by Bible stories, eager to puzzle out meanings. Church School is a time to offer them values they can take into their daily lives.

Teaching preschool is important because it is the support on which the rest of a child's religious education will be built. If a tower is to be constructed, start on a sound and broad base.

Let's Be Realistic

Most Church School teachers are not trained teachers. We're volunteers, parents, or other church members who care about children. We may have experience caring for our own children, perhaps have been baby-sitters or scout leaders. Teaching a class is a different experience. A teacher must deal with a larger group of children and must try to help those children understand a lesson. It takes preparation and energy to face a class of restless preschoolers.

Preparation and energy, two valuable commodities. Everyone is busy, running from jobs to family activities, school and chores. It is hard enough to find the time to volunteer on Sunday morning, let alone spend time preparing lessons during the week. The lessons in this book generally require little preparation. When some groundwork is required before facing the children, it is carefully spelled out in the directions. The only thing you must do before Sunday morning is take a few minutes to choose your lesson and think about how you will present it.

Money is another difficult hitch for most Church Schools. If a teacher had unlimited funds a trip to a craft store could yield plenty of fun projects for preschoolers. Most Church Schools function on a shoestring, however, so teachers must be creative with materials that are more easily found. This isn't all bad. The children learn how to make things from simple materials, rather than depending on kits. Often a craft project is also a lesson in recycling, turning milk cartons or paper plates to new uses.

Consider The Children

Preschoolers are charming and difficult, helpful and stubborn, friendly and argumentative. They change from day to day and grow faster than can be imagined.

Before starting class look over a list of children you will be teaching. Are they young preschoolers, or close to kindergarten? Have they attended Church School before? Do they know each other? Are there new children, likely to be left out or shy? If you don't know all of the children try to talk to parents or former teachers before the first day of class. If you can't do that, at least be prepared for the mix of ages and friends that you will face.

There is a big difference between the abilities of a three-year-old and those of a five-year-old. Some lessons in this book are more appropriate for younger preschoolers; others are directed at older students. Mixing children of different skills can be enriching for all involved. Older children can help younger children. Younger

8

children are challenged to try new things by watching their older friends.

Be sensitive to the differences in ability. Ask older children to do more of the cutting or lettering; younger children can glue and color. Also remember that if a five-year-old has been in your class in the past, she may be bored with the same projects or stories. Giving her more responsibility, enlisting her help in telling the story, and asking her more difficult questions can help hold her attention.

Never underestimate a child's desire to learn. Even little ones are intrigued by the ideas presented in Bible stories. I've seen three-year-olds enraged by the story of the Good Samaritan, and five-year-olds can ask surprisingly probative questions about God's presence in our world.

Preschoolers need free time. Their attention spans are short and lessons can quickly bore them. They also need time to play with each other and develop relationships. Friends can make Church School more enjoyable and keep children coming back as they grow older. The preschool class is often where such friendships start, and they are formed over dolls and blocks.

Looking Around

Take a walk through the classroom and try to look at it through the eyes of a preschooler.

Is it attractive? Is it bright enough? Are toys easily accessible and easy to clean up? Like adults, children respond to their environment. Little things can brighten up a room: a scatter rug or table cloth, some flowers or a new picture. The classroom should be a place that is comfortable and interesting.

Look over the basic supplies you have in the room. Often old or broken toys collect in a classroom, and no one takes responsibility to throw them away. Do it. Wash any toys that show the wear of many little hands. Then arrange what you have so that children can reach them easily. Put books where children can get at them as well. Even if they can't read they will enjoy looking at the pictures.

A good book of children's Bible stories is helpful. I wouldn't recommend you read the stories directly from the text, but it gives you a guideline for telling the story. Try to get a book with good illustrations. The children will enjoy looking at the pictures while you tell the story, and they can be used as models in art projects.

Basic art supplies should include:

- Paper, colored and white
- Markers and/or crayons
- Pencils
- Scissors
- Glue
- Tape

Check the supplies. Markers dry out; scissors get too dull to cut. If there is a huge bucket of crayons, throw some of them away or break them into smaller cans so children can find the color they want. Don't frustrate the children by giving them materials that don't work. These basic supplies should be kept where the students can reach them. Many children love to draw and will spend free time doing so.

Getting Parents Involved

Consider yourself a parent educator as well, and start getting them involved in the Church School. Ask them to pick their children up and take time to see what they have done that day. Occasionally plan events or lessons that directly involve parents. This may be difficult if your Church School runs at the same time as worship services, but if you give parents advance warning it will work out. You may want to consider sending a schedule of the topics you will be discussing home with each child on a monthly basis.

Having parents who are involved in your class is good for the children and for the teacher. When parents show an interest in what goes on in Church School children learn that it is important, not just baby-sitting. And if there is a problem with a child, it is easier for a teacher to talk to a parent that she knows.

Finally, if parents know what is happening in the classroom, they can discuss it with their children at home. The lessons taught in Church School are meant to be carried out into everyday life. Home is a good place to start.

Making Choices

You can't do every lesson described in this book in one year. A new topic or a new Bible story every week would be overwhelming for preschoolers. Take your time, allowing them time to talk and ask questions. Give them plenty of time to work on the art projects. Like adults, children hate to be rushed. Especially if your class is composed largely of three-year-olds, make sure to take time to relax and enjoy each other.

Caution

Teachers and parents should keep in mind that young children should be closely supervised while working on the projects in this book. Some projects use small objects, such as beans or seeds, which children might place in their ears, noses, or mouths. Other small objects, scissors, glue, plastic bags, and so forth are included in the projects. Careful supervision and caution are encouraged at all times.

Chapter Two

Breaking The Ice

The first day of Church School is exciting and nerve-wracking. It is important to get off to a good start. Even if the children already know each other, they will need to get comfortable with the school and with you. Often there will be one or two new children who may feel left out in a group of old friends. The first day should focus on ice breakers and community building.

The first day is also the day to set some ground rules. Three- to five-year-olds are able to understand and follow simple rules if they have them explained to them. Don't assume the children know what your expectations are. Taking the time to talk about classroom rules will help avoid future confusion and make the children feel more secure about their behavior. This is a good time to describe the pattern of activities you will be doing on a typical Sunday morning. When will you tell the story or do an art project? Will there be a snack? When is free play all right?

Talking Together

Although you may not want to introduce a Bible story on the first day of class, you will want to spend some time talking with the children. Use this time to let the children get to know you and to get to know them. Here are several suggestions for topics. Don't try to talk about all of these things on the first day; remember preschoolers have short attention spans.

1) Tell about yourself. Tell them your name, how old you are, whether you have children or grandchildren. Satisfy some of their curiosity. Then ask them to tell about themselves: name, age, and family.

2) Children love to hear stories about when adults were as little as them. Tell a story about something that happened to you when you were a child. Don't be afraid to embellish a little to make it more exciting. If you have a photograph of yourself as a child, bring it along to show the class.

3) Talk about the summer. Tell what you did during the summer, perhaps about a vacation you took. Then have the children tell about something they did over the summer.

4) This can be a good time to involve parents in the classroom. Contact the parents before the first day and ask them to come prepared to tell a story from their childhood. Have them bring photos of themselves as children.

5) Talk about school. Ask how many of the children attend a preschool or kindergarten. Have them tell about their schools. Then ask them how they think Church School is different. Talk about why children attend Church School and why we attend church.

6) Tour the room. You may not have much space, the children might be able to explore it quickly themselves. A tour can point out things they may not have noticed on their own and can give them a greater sense of freedom in the room. Talk about what art supplies they can use on their own, about reading books, and about cleaning up. Make sure they understand that it is their classroom.

The Working Together Story

This is a story that uses the children's names and allows them to work together to overcome a difficulty. It's noisy, especially if you have a larger group of children. You will need a balloon, a pin, and a rhythm instrument or noise maker for each child.

Once upon a time there was a church {fill in the name of your church}, and it was filled with people who worshiped together, and worked together, and played together. Some of the people were named {fill in the children's names}.

One Sunday morning when the people came to the church they found all the doors locked, and sitting on the front steps was a horrible troll. {At this point show the children a balloon on which you have drawn a mean face.}

Finally someone asked the troll why he had locked the church, and what he wanted. The troll {use the balloon as a puppet} snarled and said, "I won't let you meet here anymore. I don't like the music you make, and the sound of talking and laughing. I don't like the organ playing, or the sound of people praying together. Go away, all of you." And he snarled again in a terrifying way.

The people didn't know what to do. They were frightened. They wanted to go to church, but they didn't know how to get past the troll.

But one little {boy or girl} had been listening very carefully to what the troll had said. {Fill in the first child's name} thought about all of the things the troll had said he hated — music, laughter, the organ, and people praying together. {He/She} noticed that they were all sounds, and it gave {him/her} an idea of how to get rid of the troll.

Bravely, {First child} stepped out of the crowd. {Give the first child a rhythm instrument. Explain it is only to be played when you point at it.} {He/She} had a {name of instrument}, and {he/she} started to play it as loudly as possible. {As child plays instrument, make the balloon bounce around as if the troll is angry.}

The troll howled. He couldn't stand the noise. But he stayed on the church steps blocking the door.

{First Child} turned to {his/her} friend, {name of second child}, and said, "The troll can't stand noise. Help me make louder noise." {Give the second child an instrument, and let them both play together.}

The troll was so angry he stood up and stamped his feet, but he didn't leave the church. So the children called another friend, {Third child}, to help.

15

{Continue in this manner until all but one child have noise makers. Make sure to use the balloon, wave it around and make snarling noises to show how angry the troll is.}

The troll was so angry now that he was dancing in a circle, and smoke was coming out of his ears. His nose was turning red, and his snarly, dirty hair was standing on end. But still he blocked the church door! The children were getting tired, and they weren't sure they could make any more noise, when {Last child's name} stepped out of the crowd. "Let me help," {he/she} said.

{Have all the children play together. Then suddenly pop the balloon with the pin.} The troll disappeared in a pop, the church doors flew open, and everyone cheered.

Music

Many songs can be used as icebreakers if you use the names of the children in the words. Focus on simple, repetitive songs that the children can easily learn. Good examples are "He's Got The Whole World In His Hands," filling in "He's got Michael and Lisa, in his hands ...." or "Jesus Loves Me," filling in "Jesus loves Zach, this I know ...."

Consider learning a "class song." Choose a simple song that you will sing every Sunday together, either as a welcome or as grace before your snack. The children will love the repetition and will learn the song well. Some Sunday you may want to have them sing it in adult worship services.

Art Projects For Community Building

1) Giant Class Mural

Supplies:

> Bulletin board paper (big enough to trace children on)
> Washable markers
> A variety of multi media decorations (colored paper, ribbons, glitter)
> Glue

Gathering supplies is the only preparation necessary.

Tell the children you are going to work together to make a picture of your class. Have each child lie down on the paper and trace around him or her with a marker. You can have them lie side by side, so they appear to be standing holding hands, or let them create a more haphazard design. Allow the children to decorate their own picture, using markers or gluing whatever decoration they wish to use. Finish up by adding a title, "God's Community of Children" or "Celebrate Children." Encourage bright colors and a lot of decoration, reminding the children that it is a big space to fill in.

2) Hands and Feet

Supplies:

Bulletin board paper
Washable paint in a variety of colors
Pie tins or plastic plates
Newspapers
Buckets of water and towels

Some teacher preparation will be necessary to get your room ready for this project.

This is a messy project, but one that children really love. You might want to contact parents in the week before class and warn them to send the children in play clothes.

Before class draw pencil lines on the big paper in the shape of a rainbow. Make them dark enough that the children will see them, but light enough to be covered by paint. Cover the floor in newspaper. You might want to tape it down so it doesn't slip. Then spread the big rainbow drawing on the floor. Pour a thin layer of paint in the pie tins or plastic plates. Have a barefoot child step in a color of paint, and then carefully walk along the line, heel to toe. When he/she has run out of paint, allow a second child to finish the line. The first child should wash his/her feet in the water provided. The second line of the rainbow is done in a different color, using hand prints instead of foot prints. The third can be done with feet again.

3) Building a Tower
Supplies:
>> Empty milk cartons
>> Contac™ paper (plain white or a light color)
>> Marker that will write on the contact paper

This project involves advance planning for teachers.

Before class you have to prepare the milk cartons. The preparation for this project is more involved, but the blocks can be used in your classroom for a long time. Clean the cartons out well. Although it isn't absolutely necessary, it is a good idea to weight the blocks by putting some rice or beans inside the carton. Tape up the ends of the carton so it forms a block, and so the rice doesn't leak out. Cover the cartons with contact paper.

In class, as you introduce each child, write his/her name on a block, then give the block to the child. If you have enough blocks you can make one for the teachers, for parents, or anyone else the children might know in the church. The children can decorate the other sides of the blocks by coloring on them. Once everyone has a block, work together to build a tower. Tell the children the tower is like your church, a building made up of the people in your church community.

4) Instant Photo Mural
Supplies:
>> Poster board
>> Instant camera and film to take a picture of each child
>> Markers
>> Construction paper
>> Glue
>> Photo corners or tape

The only teacher preparation required is gathering necessary materials.

Take a picture of each child. While the photos develop, have them decorate a piece of construction paper to act as a frame for their picture. Make sure to write their name on the frame, or have them write it. Attach the photos to the construction paper frames with the photo corners or tape. Then glue the frames onto the poster board to create a class mural.

5) Classroom Photos

Throughout the year bring a camera to class and take pictures of the children working and playing together. Make sure to get a few of each child. Children love to look at pictures of themselves and their friends, and they can be used for projects later on.

Chapter Three

Adult Connections

Too often the Church School begins to feel like a separate congregation from the adult church. Creating links between the children and adults in the church builds community and makes the children feel more at home in their church. Although younger preschoolers may feel shy about actually talking with strange adults, they are curious about the workings of the adult church. Older preschoolers, or kindergartners, often enjoy meeting new people as long as they know familiar teachers are close by.

Meeting The Grown-ups

These projects are more appropriate for older preschoolers. If you have a younger class, but still want to involve adults other than parents, have the grown-ups come to the classroom. The three-year-olds will feel more comfortable on home turf.

Talking Together

1) Ask members of the church staff to talk to the children about what they do. They can explain some of their duties, and perhaps give the children a little tour of their office. Staff members may include the minister, church secretary, Church School administrator, janitor, organist. Don't forget volunteer staff members.

2) Have adults from the congregation come to the classroom and tell a story about their childhood or adventures they have had. This can be especially nice with older adults, who may otherwise have very little to do with the children. Encourage the visitor to bring photographs or memorabilia to enliven the stories.

Projects

1) Coffee Hour

This project requires advance planning and parent cooperation.

Help the children host a coffee hour for the adults. Ask the children to bring cookies or snacks. They can arrange them on plates and set a buffet table. Although you will need adults to pour coffee, the children can take turns greeting guests as they come to get their snacks.

2) People Treasures

Supplies:

Lists of "people treasures"

Instant camera (optional)

Some preparation required before Sunday class.

Have a scavenger hunt for people. Make a list of "people treasures" that the children must look for and bring back to the classroom. "People treasures" will vary, depending on the adults in your church. The list may include the minister, a man with grey hair, a doctor, the parent of a new baby, or any other easily found person. Children may be asked to either bring the person, or to take an instant photo and bring that back to the classroom.

Make sure that an adult the children feel comfortable with accompanies them on the hunt. If you have a large class, you may want to break into teams, with different lists for each team.

If you have adults brought to your classroom, have the children serve them a snack. It will give them something to do and encourage conversation. You may want to warn adults in the church that this activity will be happening, so they aren't too surprised when they are kidnapped by children.

3) Pen Pal Mail Boxes

Supplies:

Small boxes, such as shoe boxes, or large envelopes

Markers

Glitter, ribbons, colored paper for decorations

Glue

Scissors

This project requires advance planning and other adult volunteers.

Start an ongoing project for your class by having "pen pals." Line up a group of adult volunteers who agree to be pen pals with children in your class. On the first day of the project have these adults come to the class and meet the children. Have the adult and child pals make "mail boxes" together. Decorating shoe boxes works well, or if boxes are scarce, they could even decorate large envelopes. Put the children's mail boxes in their classroom, and find a place elsewhere in the church for the adult's mail boxes.

At various times in the year have the children make "mail" for their adult pen pals. Christmas cards and Valentines are obvious choices. Occasionally simply have the children draw pictures for the adults. If a pen pal is sick, encourage a get well card. Make sure adults realize that the children will be checking their mail boxes, too, and will be disappointed if they don't find mail.

4) Cooperation

Start a cooperative project with an adult volunteer. Have the children bring food for the food shelf, or help pick up the bulletins left in the sanctuary once a month. Enlist an adult to supervise the project.

Stewardship

Talking to preschoolers about stewardship can be easier than talking to adults. Preschoolers are usually eager to help, especially if they can see that they are really making a difference. Explain that Jesus asked us to help each other, and to help our Church family. Let the children talk about ways they help their families at home. Discuss ways that their parents help the Church. Explain that without all our contributions, the good work of the Church couldn't continue.

Talking Together

1) Have an offering service at the beginning of each class. Remember that children need to understand a concrete result for their offerings, so choose a specific beneficiary of their money.

For example, if your area has a program that collects toys for needy children at Christmas, direct your offerings there. Start collecting in the fall, telling the children that on December 1st you will send all the money to the charity. Make sure they understand when and where the money will go.

Tell the parents about your offering service and beneficiary. They can help to ensure that children have a nickel or dime every Sunday to contribute.

2) Instead of a money offering, start a food shelf offering in your room. Tell children to bring cans of food to class. Help them understand that the food will be given to people who are hungry. Cans of food are good visual reminders for the children. You can have a big box that the children must fill before it can be donated. Or set aside a corner of the room, mark a spot on the wall that is four or five feet high, and build a tower. Make sure to build a pyramid, so that it doesn't tip over too easily.

Tell parents you are collecting food and encourage them to send cans with their children.

3) Have an adult from the church come and talk to the children about missions. Make sure he understands that the talk should be simple and short. Use pictures to illustrate the people that your church's missions help.

Projects

1) The Church Chain
Supplies:
> Paper
> Markers
> Tape

This project requires some advance preparation.

Cut strips of paper, about an inch wide and five inches long. These will be the links of the chain. Talk about how a chain is only as strong as each of the links, just like the Church is only strong if we all work together. Write each child's name on a strip of paper. Make a circle of the first strip, taping the ends together.

Pass the second strip through the circle, and make a circle of it. Continue in this manner to make the chain.

After connecting all the children in a chain, add teachers names, parents names, and other adults the children may know. The project can be moved into the adult church by taking strips of paper to the adults and asking them to write their names. The longer the chain, the more effective the lesson.

4) The Children's Deacons

Have the class form their own "Children's Deacons." Periodically call meetings of the Board and decide on contributions that they will make to the Church. They may decide to draw pictures to contribute to the Church Newsletter, to act as greeters one Sunday, to sing in services, or to bring flowers for the sanctuary.

Prayer

Explain to the children that prayer is talking to God. There are many kinds of prayer, thanking God for what we have, letting God know we are happy, or asking for help when we are worried or sad. Talk about prayers that are memorized, like the Lord's Prayer, and those that are impromptu. Be prepared for questions about how we know that God is listening, and how God answers prayers.

Talking Together

1) Start learning a prayer together. Practice it every week. If the class is older, you may want to try the Lord's Prayer. If you do, try to explain what some of the old fashioned language means. If your class is younger, choose an easier prayer. "God is great, God is good, Thank you for our world. Amen" can be a good beginning.

2) Write a thank-you prayer together. Have the children list things that they are thankful for. Allow them to come up with ideas of their own, but discourage listing of toys. While they talk, make a list on a big piece of paper. Although they cannot read what you are writing, they will be impressed that it is being recorded.

1) Prayer Poster

Supplies:

A typed copy of a children's prayer for each student

Large pieces of paper

Glue

Markers or crayons

Minimal advance preparation required.

Read the prayer you have typed for the children. This is a good place to use the prayer they wrote themselves. Help them glue their copies of the prayer onto a larger piece of paper. Have them decorate the paper around the prayer with illustrations of what the prayer says. For example, if they thank God for the sun, have them draw a sun.

2) A Prayer Book

Supplies:

Paper

Hole puncher

Yarn

A typed copy of a children's prayer for each child

Markers or crayons

Glue

Advanced preparation required.

Before class fold the pieces of paper in half, like a bulletin. Cut the typed prayer up into separate sentences or paragraphs, depending on how long it is. This is a good time to use the prayer the children wrote themselves. Glue a sentence or paragraph on each half page of paper, so that you can put it together to make a book. Make sure you glue the sentences on the pages in the right order.

In class have the children illustrate each page. For example, if page one thanks God for the sun, have them draw a sun. When they have drawn all their pictures, help them put the pages together into a book. Punch two holes along the folded edge, lace a piece of yarn through the holes and tie it firmly.

3) Holding others in your heart

Supplies:

    Big piece of red or pink paper
    Scissors
    White paper
    Tape
    Marker

Only advance preparation required is gathering supplies.

Talk to the children about prayers we offer for other people, either those we know or those who are far away but are in need of help. Explain that praying for others is a way of showing our love for them, or holding them in our hearts.

Cut a heart out of the red or pink paper. Have the children cut the white paper into strips, or, if they are able, into smaller hearts. Have the children suggest people they want to hold in their hearts. Family members and friends will be obvious, but encourage them to think of others who need prayers as well. Write the names on the white paper strips and have the children tape them to the big heart.

Hang the heart up so that parents can read the names and talk about it with the children.

4) A Full Plate

Supplies:

    White paper plates
    Markers or crayons
    Hole puncher
    Yarn

Gathering supplies is the only advance preparation needed.

Talk with the children about the many hungry people in the world. This is an especially good prayer project if the class is collecting food for the food shelf.

With a black marker, write "Thank You, God, for a full plate." on each paper plate. Then have the children draw pictures of some of their favorite foods on the plates.

Punch a hole near the top of the plate and string a piece of yarn through it so that the plate can be hung.

5) Telephones

Supplies:

> Paper cups
> String
> Scissors

Gathering supplies is the only advance preparation needed.

This is a silly prayer project. Tell the children that prayer is like talking on the telephone, because you can't see the person you are talking to, but it doesn't mean they aren't listening.

Punch a small hole in the bottom of each paper cup. Put the string through the hole and knot it so it won't slip off. Attach another cup at the other end of the string. Make sure to put at least 3 or 4 feet of string between the cups. When a child talks into one cup a listener will be able to hear through the other end of the "telephone."

Worship Services

Children are curious about what their parents are doing in the worship services. Even if they are present during the services, they don't understand what is happening. Taking the time to explain some of the service, and to let them see the sanctuary close up, makes them feel more at home in their church.

Talking Together

1) Tour the sanctuary. Let them touch the offering plates and altar. Let them stand at the lectern. Talk with them about the decorations in the church and what they mean. Let them go in the choir loft and play the organ.

2) Attend a baptism as a class. Afterwards talk with them about their own baptisms. Explain what baptism means in your Church. Contact parents in advance and ask them to send along pictures of their child's baptism.

3) Show them the communion cups and plates. Explain how communion is a time for remembering Jesus and the last time he ate a meal with his friends. If your Church allows children to participate in communion, ask the minister to come to the classroom and offer a special communion with the children. As she does so she can take time to explain what she is doing in more detail than she does during an adult service.

Projects

1) Stained Glass Windows
Supplies:
> Waxed paper
> Crayon pieces
> Colored paper
> Iron
> Newspapers

This project requires some advance preparation.

Before class chop the crayon pieces up into fine bits. Keep the colors separate in paper cups or plastic bags.

Give each child two pieces of waxed paper, about the same size as a piece of construction paper. Have them carefully arrange crayon bits on the waxy side of one sheet. Place the second sheet, waxy side down, on top of the crayon bits.

Put the waxed paper on a sheet of newspaper, with another newspaper on top. Have an adult pass over the paper with a warm iron, until the crayons are melted. Keep a close eye on the progress; the crayons can quickly turn to a soupy mess.

Allow the papers to cool for a couple minutes. In the meantime cut frames out of the construction paper. Fold each piece in half and cut out a rectangle in the middle, leaving about an inch of frame on all sides. Have the children tape their crayon picture to the frame. Show them how the light shines through, illuminating the colors.

2) Baking Bread

Supplies:

Prepared bread dough

Small bread pans

Two cups of flour

Margarine for greasing the pans

Gathering supplies, and access to an oven is necessary.

Talk with the children about the bread that is used in communion. Tell them you are going to make your own bread.

Frozen bread dough, thawed and allowed to rise once, works well for this project. Give each child a pan and have them grease it well with some of the margarine. Then give them each a chunk of bread dough. Sprinkle some flour on the table in front of them, and show them how to knead. Allow them to squish the bread dough for a while. Then help them form loaves for their pans.

Let the children watch as you put it in the hot oven. Set a timer, and let them watch as you take them out.

The children may want to take their bread home. However, talk to your pastor beforehand about using the bread for communion. If it is used in Church, make sure to let the children know about it so they can attend.

3) Banners

Supplies:

Colored paper

Scissors

Markers

Glue

Templates of religious symbols

Thin dowels

Some preparation is necessary.

Check with your church secretary to see if templates may be available of some basic symbols. If not, cut some out of a stiff poster board or cardboard. A cross, a fish, a dove, or an angel are good examples.

Talk with the children about the banners that hang in your church and the symbols on them.

Give each child a sheet of colored paper. Then show them how to trace a symbol from a template onto a different colored paper. Help them cut out the symbol and glue it onto their banner paper. If they want they can add decorations with markers.

Glue the banner paper onto a thin dowel to form the top and a way for the children to hang the banners.

Chapter Four

God's Creation

Talking Together

The creation story (Genesis 1:1—2:3) can be a fun story to tell. The opportunities for use of props is as limitless as the natural world, and how long you want to keep talking. Here are some simple suggestions for keeping little ones' attention.

In the beginning was darkness. Make the room dark. If the class is brave, you could turn off all the lights. Then turn them on again for the creation of light. If the class is younger and more tentative, get huddled together on the floor and cover everyone in a blanket for darkness; throw off the blanket for light.

A prop bag is invaluable during story telling. Pull out a ball to illustrate the Earth. Pass it around so that each child can press it into shape. Have toy birds, fish, and animals inside the bag that can be produced at the appropriate moment, and photographs of the ocean and of the desert to illustrate water and land. Finally, reach in and pull out a lump of clay. Form it roughly into the shape of a person, and blow on it for the creation of humans.

After telling the story of creation, encourage the children to talk about all the wonderful things in God's creation. Have the children name all the animals they can think of; talk about the variety and interdependence of the animals. Talk about the seasons. Talk about trees, how they grow from tiny seeds, how long they can live, and how big they can get. Give the children time to talk about their own experiences.

Music

"He's Got The Whole World In His Hands" using a different day of creation for each verse. [He's got the darkness and the light, in his hands ...] This is an easy song for the kids to learn.

"All Things Bright And Beautiful" takes more practice, but an older class can learn it.

Art Projects Focusing On The Natural World
1) Earthy Coasters
Supplies:
>Flour
>Salt
>Oil
>Water
>A bunch of small rocks, or acorns, or shells
>Masking tape

Requires advance teacher preparation.

For the clay: Mix 4 cups of flour and 1 cup of salt. Mix 2 tbsp. of vegetable oil into 1 cup of water. Stir the water into the flour and salt mixture. Knead together, adding small amounts of water until you get a smooth clay. If it gets too sticky, add a little more flour.

Make a ring shaped mold out of masking tape. Rip off a piece of tape about 24 inches long. Carefully fold the tape in half, sticky sides together, with about an inch of sticky tape left at the end. Make a circle out of the tape, using the sticky end to tape it together. You should have a circle of masking tape that is not sticky at all. Don't expect the kids to make the circle since sticky tape is frustrating for little hands to deal with.

Give each child a mold, and an egg sized ball of clay. Have them put the clay in the middle of the ring, and press it flat. Then they can use the rocks, acorns, shells or whatever to decorate the clay. Make sure they press the decorations firmly into the clay. Let the coasters dry in the molds until the next class. Remove the tape and they are ready to go.

2) Autumn Leaf Collages
Supplies:
>Collection of dry leaves
>Waxed paper
>An iron

Newspapers
Construction paper
Scissors

Gathering supplies is the only preparation necessary.

This is an oldie but a goodie. Let the children choose some leaves and arrange them on pieces of waxed paper. The waxed paper should be about the same size as a piece of construction paper, and the leaves need to be in the center of the waxed paper. Place another piece of waxed paper on top of the leaves, waxy sides together. Place newspapers under the waxed paper, and on top. With a warm, not hot, iron, have an adult press the waxed paper. The waxed paper will melt together, sealing in the leaves.

Fold a piece of construction paper in half and cut a square out of the middle, leaving about a 2 inch wide frame of paper around the outside. This will be a frame for the leaf collage. Tape the waxed paper to the frame for a finished look that covers the rough edges of the waxed paper.

3) Leaf Rubbing
Supplies:
> Flat, dry leaves
> White paper, preferably like typing paper
> Crayons
> Tape

Gathering supplies is the only advance preparation necessary.

Have each child select a leaf. Tape the leaf loosely to a piece of paper. Show the children how to hold the side of the crayon flat to the paper and rub. Place the leaf side of the paper flat on a table, tape the paper to the table. Have the children rub over the leaf.

4) Seed Pictures
Supplies:
> A variety of dry seeds and beans (sunflower seeds in the shell, lentils, red beans, rice)
> Construction paper
> Glue
> Pencils

Gathering supplies is the only preparation necessary.

Draw an outline of a simple design or picture on the paper. A basic religious symbol like a cross or fish works well. Place the seeds out in separate small dishes around the children's table. Tell the children to work in small areas, so that the glue doesn't dry before they have a chance to decorate it. Smear glue over a small area, and fill in the space with the seeds. Make sure to use plenty of glue, and leave the pictures flat long enough to get dry.

5) Tissue Paper Butterflies
Supplies:
Colored tissue paper
Construction paper
White vinegar
An eye dropper
Newspaper

Gathering supplies is the only preparation necessary.

Fold a piece of construction paper in half and cut a butterfly wing-shaped hole along the fold. When you unfold the paper you will have two wings. Allow the children to choose a sheet of colored tissue paper. Tape the tissue paper behind the butterfly opening. Place the butterfly on the newspaper because in the next step the colors will run. Have the children carefully place a few drops of vinegar onto the tissue paper. The colors in the paper will run, creating a design. Let it dry for a few minutes. Cut a cigar shape out of brown construction paper, slightly longer than the butterfly. This will be the butterfly's body. Allow the children to draw a face on their butterfly body. Then glue the body over the dried tissue paper butterfly. The colors will show best if the butterfly is hung on a window.

6) Creation Mural
Supplies:
Large sheet of white paper
Large sheet of blue paper
Yellow paper

Small pieces of sponge
White paint
Magazines for pictures of animals and people
Glue
Scissors

Some advance work is necessary.

Cut a circle out of the blue paper. It needs to be big enough to allow the children to glue animals and people onto it. Glue the circle into the center of the large white paper. This is the Earth. Let a couple of children use the white paint and sponges to sponge paint some clouds across the surface of the Earth. Cut a sun, moon, and a couple stars out of the yellow paper and glue them on either side of the planet. When the paint is dry let the children cut pictures from the magazine of animals, plants, and people and glue them on the Earth.

7) The Church Tree

Supplies:
Big sheet of white paper
Big sheet of brown paper
Construction paper
Glue
Scissors

Some preparation required.

Before class cut a tree shape, trunk and branches out of the brown paper. Glue it onto the white paper. Tell the children this is the tree of your church, and just like God puts the leaves on the tree, God also puts the people in your church.

You will need enough paper cut into leaves to cover the tree. If you have some older children in your group (5-year-olds), they can help you do the cutting. If your group is made up of younger children, you should probably cut the leaves in advance. First write the names of the children in your class on the leaves. If the children can write their own names, let them. Have them glue the leaves onto the tree. Then you can write the parents' and siblings' names on the tree. Finally branch out into other people they might know in the church.

When you have a tree full of leaves, you can embellish the picture with birds, a sun, grass around the bottom of the tree or a squirrel. Let the children come up with ideas.

8) Seasons Murals

Supplies:

> Bulletin board paper
> Markers or crayons
> Paint
> Construction paper
> Scissors
> Glue and tape

No preparation required.

Murals representing the seasons can be an ongoing project for the class. At the beginning of each new season talk about how it is part of God's creation. Talk about how plants grow in summer, and rest in winter. Talk about how the falling leaves decay and enrich the soil. Then talk about things the children enjoy doing in the season. Give them a big piece of bulletin board paper and let them create a scene, swimming in summer, snowmen in winter. The mural can decorate the room until the next season begins.

Chapter Five

Old Testament Stories

Most three- to five-year-old children have not had much exposure to Bible stories before starting Church School. To avoid confusion in their minds it is easiest to focus their attention on "Jesus stories." There are, however, a few Old Testament stories that are especially fascinating to young children.

Noah's Ark

The story of Noah's ark (Genesis 6-9) has always been a favorite of children because of the image of a ship full of animals. Yet, it can be difficult to describe the angry God of Noah without sounding frightening. Use the story to discuss the importance of listening to God, and the benefits of trying to live up to God's expectations for us.

Art Projects

1) Animal Masks
Supplies:

>Stiff paper, such as tag board or poster board *or* paper plates
>Popsicle sticks or plastic straws
>Markers or crayons
>Scissors
>Glue

Some advance preparation is necessary.

Out of the stiff paper cut a circle for each child, large enough to cover their faces. Using a dinner plate as a guide should give you a good size and shape. The paper plates may be used instead of these circles.

In class, have the children talk about the animals that went on Noah's ark. Have each child choose an animal. Then give them the circles and tell them they will be making masks.

An adult should cut the eye holes in the mask. Hold the circle in front of the child's face in order to approximate how far apart the holes should be cut. If the child is making an animal where the ears are an important part of the design you may want to help them. By placing the eye holes a bit further down on the circle there will be room at the top to cut out ears for a cat or fox.

After the cutting is done have the children decorate the masks with markers. If you have animal pictures in books or magazines let the children look at them as they color. It will help keep them on track. If a mask needs a horn or trunk you can cut it out of construction paper and glue it on.

Finally, glue a popsicle stick to the bottom of the mask as a handle. If you are using straws you will probably need to tape it on instead.

2) Noah's Mural
Supplies:
> Large bulletin board paper
> Paint and brushes
> Either smaller pieces of paper and markers or a collection
> > of animal magazines
> Tape
> Scissors

Some advance preparation required.

The amount of work you need to do before class for this project depends upon the age of your students. Sketch an ark on the big piece of paper, making sure it is sitting in water. If your class includes some four- and five-year-olds, they can paint the ship and background in. If the class is mostly three-year-olds, paint the ark scene in before class. Make sure paint is dry before you try to glue to it.

Consider the abilities of your class. If they like to draw let them make pictures of animals on the smaller pieces of paper, cut them out and tape or glue them to the ark. Give them pictures of animals to look at while they work. If they aren't up to that big a project, let them cut pictures of animals out of magazines and attach them to the ark. Either way, try to get a wide variety of animals and really crowd the ship.

3) Milk Carton Ark
Supplies:
> Empty milk cartons, well washed
> A sharp kitchen knife
> Plastic straws
> Construction paper
> Animal crackers or animal stickers

Some preparation is necessary.

Use the sharp knife to cut each milk carton in half. Milk cartons make great boats because they float. However, the same waxy paper that allows them to float makes them hard to decorate, so don't have the children try to paint them.

Make a slit in one end of each straw, about an inch long. These will be used to support the sail. Have the children cut sails out of the construction paper, about as wide as the milk carton. They can use markers to make pictures on their sails if they wish. Then have them tape a straw to each side of the sail. Make sure the sail is attached to the end of the straw that is not slit. Slip the slit end of the straw over the sides of the milk carton to create a sail.

The simplest way to put animals in the ark is to use animal crackers. Make sure to have a lot of them, since they will get eaten. Another more permanent method is to put animal stickers on construction paper, then have the children cut out the stickers. These create paper dolls that can be put in the ark.

If you have a big sink or large water bucket you can let the children take turns sailing their arks.

4) Animal Hats
Supplies:
> Newspaper
> Construction paper in a variety of colors

Scissors

Glue

Some preparation is necessary, depending on the age of students.

Three-year-olds are unable to fold their own hats, but five-year-olds are often able to follow along with you. Decide if you need to fold hats in advance, or whether you can do it in class.

To make a hat

1. Start with a double sheet of newspaper, creased in the middle as if you are going to read. Have the fold at the top, away from you.

2. Fold the upper corners down and to the middle. They will meet about two to three inches above the bottom of the paper. You now have a triangle top to your paper.

3. Fold the bottom edge of the top sheet of paper up to meet the bottom edge of your triangle. Fold this up again so that it overlaps the triangle by about an inch, and you have a double folded border at the bottom of your hat.

4. Turn the hat over. Fold the bottom outer edges in so that they meet at the middle.

5. Take the unfolded edge of paper at the bottom of your hat and fold it up so that it is even with the other bottom edge. It should extend above your border by about an inch. Tuck this inch into the border. This will anchor your hat so that it stays together.

6. The hat can be worn with a pointed top, as it is now, or you can fold the top down and tuck the point into the bottom border for a square topped hat.

Practice making a hat a couple times before class. Once you get the hang of it, hats are very easy to make.

Let the children cut eyes, ears, noses, and so forth, out of construction paper and glue them to the hats. It works well to have the ears stick up at the top, and try to get the nose firmly across the front. The children can color on the hats with markers as well.

Tails can also be a nice touch. Poke a hole at the back of the hat, run a piece of heavy yarn through it and knot each end so that it won't slip out.

5) Ark Collages

Supplies:

> Collection of animal magazines
> Construction paper
> Glue
> Scissors

Gathering supplies is the only preparation necessary.

Make an ark shaped piece of paper by cutting two corners off a piece of construction paper. Make the cuts slightly curved, like the bottom of a ship. Children can do this themselves if you draw them pencil guidelines.

Tell the children this is their ark which they need to fill with animals. Let them cut pictures out of the magazines and glue them to their ark. Encourage them to overlap and really fill the ark.

The Baby Moses

The story of the baby put in a basket (Exodus 1-4) is an introduction to Moses and the conflict between the Israelites and the Egyptians. Although the Pharaoh's order to kill Israelite baby boys is a harsh beginning to the story, it illustrates the horrors of slavery very clearly to the children. If you tell them about it simply, and don't dwell on the horror, it need not be frightening. Explain how Moses is saved because God plans for him to save his people.

Art Projects

1) Baby in a Basket Pictures

Supplies:

> Construction paper, blue, green, brown and tan
> Scissors
> Glue

Some preparation required, depending on the age of the class.

If your class is younger, you will need to cut the various parts of the picture out for them. If the class is older, draw guidelines and let them do the cutting themselves.

From the green paper cut a jagged border to represent the reeds and grasses in the river. It should be as wide across as the piece of construction paper, and three or four inches high.

From the brown paper cut a basket. Two half ovals, about four inches long and two inches high, is fine.

The baby Moses should be cut from the tan paper. Make the outline of a swaddled baby by having a larger oval shape with a small circle on one end for the head. The children can use crayons to color the blanket and add the baby's face. The baby figure should be sized appropriately to fit into the basket.

Use a full piece of blue paper as the background. Below the grass it is the river, above the grass it is sky. Glue the grass onto the blue paper along the bottom and sides. This leaves a pocket in the middle where the basket can be placed.

Glue two basket pieces together along the curved edge. Leave the top edge open, creating an envelope where the baby can be placed.

Once the glue is dry, slip the baby into the basket, and the basket behind the reeds for a Moses picture.

2) Peanut Babies

Supplies:

      Peanuts in the shell

      Egg cartons

      Pieces of scrap fabric

      Markers

Gathering supplies is only preparation necessary.

Cut the egg carton apart. Each egg cup can be used as a basket for the peanut baby. Have the children color them brown.

Help the children glue a piece of scrap fabric around the peanut to look like a blanket wrapped around a baby. Leave the "head" out so that the children can draw Moses's face on with a marker.

Place the peanut baby in the egg carton basket.

3) Clay Baby in a Basket

Supplies:

      Clay (as described on page 34)

      Access to an oven

      Paint and brushes

Clay should be made in advance.

Give each child a ball of clay about the size of an orange. Have them make a pinch pot, by pressing their thumbs into the middle of the ball and pinching the sides out. This will be the basket. Next give them a ball of clay about the size of a ping pong ball. Have them roll it between their hands for a moment, to make it into an egg shape. This will be the baby.

While the children have a free time, bake the clay pieces in a 250 degree oven until they are dry and hard. This should take about 15 to 20 minutes. Watch that they don't burn. Once the clay is baked the children can paint their figures. The baskets can be painted brown. Have them paint a blanket on the baby, and then a face and hair.

Exodus

The story of the plagues brought upon Egypt and the Israelites' escape from slavery (Exodus 5-14) is exciting. It also can be used to illustrate how God helps people fight for what is right, and how Moses's faith gives him the power to free his people. Don't dwell on some of the more ugly plagues in too great detail.

Older children may like to do some play acting with this story. Cast a mean pharaoh, a persistent Moses, and his brother Aaron. Let the other children take on different roles as is needed, as Israelites, or as frogs or locusts.

Music

The old spiritual "Go Down, Moses" is an obvious musical choice. Have an adult sing the verses, but teach the children the chorus. They especially like to "Tell Old Pharaoh To Let My People Go."

Art Projects

1) Snake Sticks
> Supplies:
>> Newspapers
>> Tape
>> Green felt

Scraps of black and red felt
Glue
Scissors
Tape

Advance cutting is helpful, but not necessary.

Using 5 or 6 sheets of newspaper, roll them into a tight stick. Tape the edges so that they stay together. You can use a dowel for the stick if you want to be fancier, but it also makes a dangerous weapon. Newspaper sticks really can't hurt anyone, even if they don't look quite as nice.

Cut the green felt into long, thin strips for the snakes. Have the children glue their snakes to the sticks, winding around from bottom to top. Then, using the red and black felt scraps, let them add eyes and a forked tongue.

2) Pharaoh Masks

Supplies:

Stiff paper such as tag board or poster board *or* paper plates
Popsicle sticks or plastic straws
Construction paper
Markers

Some advance preparation necessary.

Cut circles out of the stiff paper, about the size of a dinner plate, or use the paper plates. These will be the pharaoh's face. Cut eye holes after holding the circle up to the child's face to mark the approximate placing.

The most distinctive thing about a pharaoh for most children is the distinctive head scarf he is pictured wearing. Make sure you have a picture of a pharaoh for them to look at. Your Bible stories book will probably have one, otherwise get a book about King Tut from the library. Using construction paper, cut a pharaoh's hat that will fit around the mask face and glue it on. Let the children use markers to finish their face and decorate the hat.

Glue popsicle sticks to the bottom of the mask as a handle, or tape straws.

3) Parting the Red Sea

Supplies:
> A shoe box for each child
> Blue construction paper
> Stiff paper, tag board or poster board
> Markers
> Glue

Gathering supplies is the only preparation necessary.

The children will be making a simple diorama inside the shoe box of the Israelites escaping through the Red Sea.

Cut rectangles, about 1 inch wide by 3 inches tall, from the stiff paper. Fold over the bottom inch. Make two or three for each child. Have them draw people on these rectangles. Glue them by the bent flap to the middle of the inside of the box. The people should face the narrow end of the box.

Next, give each child two sheets of blue construction paper slightly smaller than the shoe box. Explain that although it is called the Red Sea, the water is blue. Show the children how to fold the paper like a fan.

Glue one fan to each narrow end inside the shoe box. The fans will meet in the middle. Push the figures of the "Israelites" flat to the bottom of the box, and the fans will cover them. When the glue is dry the children can push back the fans and expose the dry land underneath the sea. The people should pop up when the water is moved.

Jonah and the Whale

The story of Jonah (Jonah 1-4) illustrates the importance of listening to God and trying to live up to God's plans for you. Talk with the children about times they had a task to do, but they tried to avoid it. Explain that God doesn't talk to us directly, but that we may have to listen very carefully to our own brains and hearts to know what God wants for us.

47

1) Jonah and the Whale Game
Supplies:
> White paper cups
> Yarn or string
> Needle, big enough for the yarn
> Large beads
> Markers

Gathering supplies is the only preparation needed.

Explain to the children that they will be making a game where the whale catches Jonah. Give them each a cup. This is the whale. The mouth of the cup is the mouth of the whale. Let them decorate their whales, adding eyes and flippers. Have each child string a big bead onto a piece of yarn. The yarn should be about 10 to 12 inches long. Tie a knot at the end, so that the bead won't slip off. Next, use the needle to poke the yarn through the bottom of the cup, and knot it there as well. The bead is Jonah.

To play the game the children hold the cup and swing the yarn, trying to catch the bead inside the cup.

2) Whale Hats
Supplies:
> Large pieces of paper
> Markers
> Stapler
> Scissors

No advance preparation needed.

Each child will need two sheets of paper. Have them draw a whale shape, big enough to fit over their head, on one sheet. Bring a picture of a whale into class for them to look at while they draw. Then help them cut it out of both pieces of paper, so that there are two matching whales. If the class is younger you may have to precut the whale shapes and have them start the project with decorating.

Staple the two matching whales together all around three sides, but leaving an opening at the bottom that is big enough to fit over the child's head. Try it on and make sure the hat fits.

Let the children finish their hats by decorating the whales. They can use markers to draw eyes and fins. If there is time they could paint them first, then add details in marker. As an added touch, a little Jonah figure could be attached to the whale's mouth by a piece of yarn.

3) Big Ears for Listening
Supplies:
>Stiff paper, paper plates work well
>Construction paper
>Stapler
>Markers
>Scissors

No advance preparation needed.

The children will be making big ears to help them listen for God's directions. This is a silly project that the children will enjoy.

Have the children cut two circles out of the stiff paper, about the size of a grapefruit. Let them study each others ears and draw ears on the circles of paper.

Cut strips of construction paper, about 1 1/2 inches wide, to fit snugly around each child's head. Staple them so that they look like head bands. Then either staple or glue the children's big ears to the sides of the head band.

Chapter Six

Advent, Christmas, And Epiphany

This is the most exciting time of year for small children. Be prepared for short attention spans and wild children. As Christmas approaches make time to allow each child a chance to tell something about festivities at home. After the big day, let the children tell about one gift that they got. Allowing them to take turns can help control some of their desire to talk, and to get off subject.

Children are bombarded with the secular, consumer Christmas everywhere they go. Santa and Rudolph are wonderful, but the children will learn about them at home, from television, in books, and at stores. Save Church School for Jesus and try to really stress the religious meaning of Christmas while they are there.

Advent

Watch your calendar! Most of us don't really want to start thinking about Christmas until December, but Advent usually starts in November. In Church School Advent passes quickly; it is only four Sundays. During that time there is a lot of getting ready for the baby Jesus to do, so think ahead.

On the first Sunday in Advent tell the children about the angel's visitation of Mary. You don't want to get into the facts of life with preschoolers, but explain that the angel told Mary that she would have God's special baby. The first Sunday is a good time to bring out a creche. Ideally, the classroom creche should be made of something the children can touch and play with. Don't put the baby Jesus in the manager yet. Tell the children that Jesus won't be there till Christmas, and that Advent is the time for waiting for Jesus.

On the next three Sundays tell the story of Mary's and Joseph's trip to Bethlehem, about the crowds in Bethlehem and how there was no room for them, and of the birth in the stable. Tell them about the shepherds, but remember to save the kings for Epiphany. Most of them will have heard the story before, but it is one we all can listen to many times. Break it up over the weeks, and don't be afraid to embellish. How tired was Mary; how bumpy was the ride on the donkey? How crowded was Bethlehem, and how worried was Joseph about finding a place to stay? What was the stable like? These details bring a simple story to life for children.

Music

Choose simple Christmas carols to start singing during Advent. "Away in the Manger" is especially appealing to small children. "Go Tell It On The Mountain" is fun; let the children accompany you on rhythm instruments. For older children try teaching them each a verse from "The Friendly Beasts." It can be worked into a little play if you make animal masks.

Art Projects For Advent

1) Two Advent Calendars
Calendar one
Supplies:

> Construction paper, dark blue, brown and green
> Star stickers or a supply of small stars cut out of yellow paper
> One bigger star cut out of yellow paper
> Envelopes
> Scissors
> Glue

Gathering supplies is the only preparation needed.

The Advent calendars available in stores actually keep track of the days in December, not the days in Advent. Make an accurate one in Church School by counting the number of days from the first Sunday in Advent until Christmas.

Use the dark blue paper as background for the night sky. Have the children cut a strip of green paper and glue it to the bottom to represent the ground. Using the brown paper have them make a stable. Let them make it like a simple house. Cut a square, then cut a triangle for the roof. Glue the stable to the middle of the paper.

Count out the small stars, one for each day in Advent. Put them in the envelope. Put one big star in each envelope to be added on Christmas. The children should take their calendars home and put one small star on every day.

Calendar two
Supplies:
>   Construction paper
>   Scissors
>   Glue, tape or stapler

No preparation necessary.

This is a simple calendar that marks the days till Christmas well for younger children. Remember to count the actual number of days in Advent, not the days in December.

Cut the paper into inch wide strips. If the children are able to write numbers, have them number the strips of paper. There should be one strip for each day in Advent.

Make a paper chain by forming a circle out of the first strip of paper, then adding links.

The children take the chain home, and on each day they can rip one paper link off. As Christmas approaches their chains will get shorter and shorter.

2) Book of Jesus Stories
Supplies:
>   Paper, white and colored
>   Stapler
>   Markers or crayons

For younger classes, some preparation is needed.

Advent is a good time to start an ongoing project with the class. Making their own book will help them remember the stories about Jesus that they will hear in Church School. Since the birth is the first Jesus story, it is a good starting place.

Make the books by folding several sheets of white paper in half and putting them together like pages. Remember to make plenty of pages for the stories to come. Fold a piece of colored paper in half for the cover. Put the cover around the pages and staple the folded edge.

Have each child draw a picture of the angel visiting Mary, and of the stable or the baby Jesus. Control them; they could probably fill the whole book with Christmas pictures.

Have a special place in the classroom where you save these books, then take them out when they are ready to add the next picture. At the end of the year they will have books to take home.

3) Christmas Cards
Supplies:
>Paper in a variety of colors
>Markers and crayons
>Scissors
>Glue
>Any other decorations, glitter, stickers, old Christmas cards to cut up
>List of people in the church to send cards to

Getting mailing list is the only preparation needed.

Show the children the list of people you need to make cards for. These people could be shut ins, their pen pals, the church staff, their parents, or anyone else. If they are people children have never met, try to get pictures of them to show.

Then let them go wild. Show them how to fold the paper in half, like a card, but otherwise let them use their own imagination. Encourage them to make a variety of cards and sign their names.

If you have photos of the children, include them in the cards they have made. The children will be proud of their creation, and the receiver will enjoy seeing the child who made it.

4) A Christmas Tree Mural
Supplies:
>Large piece of bulletin board paper
>Green paint and brushes

Construction paper, magazines, old Christmas cards
Glue and tape
Glitter, sequins, ribbons, or any other fun decoration
Some advance preparation needed.

This is a fun project for children, and makes a lively Christmas decoration for the room.

Before class sketch a big Christmas tree on the bulletin board paper. Have the children work together to paint it green. It is easiest to have the paper on the floor for painting.

While the tree dries let the kids begin making decorations. Cut out balls from construction paper; add glitter or sequins. Cut out animals or toys from the magazines, and pictures from the Christmas cards.

When the tree is dry, hang it on the wall and let the children tape their decorations on.

5) Christmas Card Holder
Supplies:
Paper plates
Either stapler or paper punch and yarn
Markers
Old Christmas cards
Glue

Gathering supplies is only preparation needed.

Each child will need two paper plates. The harder white ones work best. Cut one paper plate in half. Place the two plates together with the tops facing each other. This creates a pocket between the plates. If your class is younger, simply staple the two plates together. If your class is older, help them punch holes around the edge of the two plates, then lace the yarn tightly through the holes to hold them together. This is trickier, but more attractive. You could use Christmas ribbon instead of yarn for a nice touch.

Once the pocket is formed the children may decorate the holder.

Punch a hole in the top and attach some yarn to hang the holder up.

6) Christmas Decorations
Glittery Pine Cones
Supplies:

> Pine cones, the big hard kind
> Glue
> Glitter
> Yarn

Gathering supplies is only preparation needed.

Have the children dribble glue on the pine cone. Make sure to use a glue that dries clear. Then have them sprinkle glitter in the glue. Watch out, glitter is messy, so put down newspapers before you start. Let the pine cones dry, then shake off the excess glitter. Tie yarn around the middle of the cone to create a circle to hang the decoration.

Cotton Ball Sheep
Supplies:

> Stiff paper, tag board or poster board
> Glue
> Cotton balls
> Scissors
> Paper punch
> Yarn

Some preparation needed.

Before class cut sheep shapes out of the stiff paper. Make them around four inches long and high, to allow plenty of room for cotton balls. If the class is older, you may simply draw the sheep on the paper and let them cut it out themselves.

Punch a hole in the top of the sheep before the children start gluing.

Let the children cover the sheep with cotton balls. Have them leave the faces uncovered so that they can draw eyes and mouth. Let the glue dry.

String yarn through the hole to hang the decoration.

Styrofoam Balls

Supplies:

> A Styrofoam ball for each child
> A variety of decorations, sequins, glitter, stars, ribbons, old Christmas cards
> Glue
> Straight pins
> Ribbon

Gathering supplies is the only preparation needed.

Let the children decorate the ball. Use glue for glitter, but generally attaching decorations with straight pins will anchor things better to a Styrofoam ball. Watch little ones with pins.

Cut a piece of ribbon about five inches long. Use a pin to attach the ribbon in a loop to the top of the ball as a hanger.

Silver Stars

Supplies:

> Stars cut out of stiff paper or cardboard
> Aluminum foil
> Paper punch
> Yarn or ribbon

Gathering supplies is only preparation needed.

If the children are younger cut the stars in advance for them. Older children will be able to cut their own stars if you help them draw them.

Give each child a piece of aluminum foil large enough to wrap around their star. It should cover both sides so that it stays firmly wrapped. Let them wrap the stars. They may need help getting it to lay smoothly around the points.

Punch a hole in the top of the star and string yarn or ribbon through it as a holder.

7) Christmas Wreaths

Supplies:

> Green construction paper
> Christmas ribbons
> Scraps of red and green felt *or* construction paper

Glitter

Glue

Stapler

Some preparation needed.

The children will make wreaths for their bedroom doors. Cut wreath circles out of the green paper in advance. Make them slightly larger than a dinner plate.

Help the children decorate their wreaths. Attach ribbon bows to the bottom with the stapler. Cut holly berries and leaves out of the felt and glue them on. Across the top write the child's name in glue and let them sprinkle glitter on it. When it is dry shake off the extra glitter.

Christmas

Chances are that you won't see the children on Christmas, but if you do, a Birthday Party can be a fun way to pass the time. The children will be so excited that craft projects wouldn't work anyway. Have a birthday cake for Jesus, balloons, and party hats. Play some games. Don't forget to sing "Happy Birthday" to Jesus.

Epiphany

Celebrating Epiphany, or the arrival of the kings, is a good way to wind down the Christmas holiday.

Explain to the children that Jesus's star didn't start shining until he was born. Since the Kings were coming from far away it took them a while to get to Bethlehem. The day they arrived is called Epiphany. Explain that Jesus was still in the stable because a woman needs time to rest after having a baby.

Talk with them about what gifts they would give a new baby. Then talk about why the kings brought gold, frankincense, and myrrh. Explain that they were showing respect to a new leader by bringing gifts of great value.

Music

Sing "We Three Kings." The children won't have time to learn the whole thing, but will enjoy the story. Find three men to come sing the verses and be the three kings.

Art Projects

1) Crowns

Supplies:
> Construction paper
> Stapler
> Glitter
> Glue
> Scissors
> Markers

No preparation needed.

Fit the construction paper around the child's head and cut it to the appropriate length. You will need long paper, or you will have to attach two pieces together. When you have the size right let the child cut the shape of the crown, with points and bumps. Then let them decorate with markers and glitter.

Finally, staple the back of the crown so that it fits the child's head.

2) Gift Boxes

Supplies:
> A collection of small boxes and bottles
> Glue
> Variety of decorations, glitter, sequins, ribbons, stickers
> Food coloring (optional)

Gathering supplies is the only preparation needed.

Let the children decorate gift boxes for the valuable presents the kings brought the baby Jesus. Boxes may be covered with all sorts of decorations. Bottles, for the myrrh, can be decorated on the outside. If the bottle is clear and has a good snug top, fill it with water colored with food coloring.

Chapter Seven

Jesus Stories

The children attending a Church School program will have heard of Jesus, but don't assume they know much about him. Take some time to give them some background information to work with. If you have access to a globe show the children where Israel is in relationship to their own home. Talk about how long it would take to get there.

Talk to them about the weather in Israel. Explain that it is hot and dry. Bring in some pictures to show them. The children's section at your library will have some picture books about Middle Eastern countries.

Look at Bible pictures and talk about how people are dressed. Ask the children what they wear in hot weather (shorts and t-shirts). Talk about the wind and sand in Israel, and how that would affect the clothes people wore. Also explain that people have different ideas about what clothes are proper. People in Jesus' time would have thought shorts were "bad manners." I always tell the children that as a girl I was not allowed to wear pants to school, even in the winter. You may have a similar memory that can help them understand social expectations about clothes.

Jesus walked everywhere. Look at a map of Israel and see how far it is from Jerusalem to Bethlehem or some other city. Give them a familiar reference point from your home and ask if they would like to walk there. Talk about how people got around in ancient times.

Finally, talk about Jesus' poverty. Explain that Joseph was a carpenter, and that Jesus probably learned the trade from his father. Jesus is remembered as a teacher, however, and he didn't get paid for that. Talk about how he would have lived, where he would get food and a place to sleep.

Once the children have a grasp on the time and place the Jesus stories are set in, you are ready to move on.

The Boy in the Temple

Talking Together:

The story of Jesus talking with the elders in the temple (Matthew 2:19-23; Luke 2:40-52) is important for children because it is the only picture we have of Jesus as a child. Although Jesus was older than the preschoolers, they can relate to a lot in the story. Talk about how worried Mary and Joseph must have been when they couldn't find their son. Ask if any of the children were ever lost, and how their parents reacted. Ask how they feel when they have a good, serious talk with adults, a talk where grown-ups seriously pay attention to what they think. Talk about why Jesus was so wise at such a young age.

Have a big piece of paper and a marker handy. Ask the children what they would say to the adults in their church about how to treat each other. Write down their comments and questions. Have them typed up, and either send them home so the children can talk with their parents about the comments, or include them in the church newsletter. Giving their thoughts adult attention teaches the children that what they think and feel is valuable. And remember, adults can learn from the children as well.

Art Projects

1) Carpentry project

Supplies:

      Adult helpers (perhaps parents)

      Precut and sanded wood pieces

      Tools

An ambitious, but special project. A lot of adult work is needed.

Involving the children in a simple carpentry project can be a great experience for them. It is, however, a difficult job, especially for three-year-olds. I've done pounding and cutting with preschoolers and they enjoy it a great deal. Have an adult volunteer for each child, either a parent or the church pen pal.

Choose a simple project like a stool. Have the wood pieces pre-cut and sanded so that all the children need to do is pound it together. For three-year-olds you may even want to work with wood glue. The result will not be a family heirloom, but will be a source of great pride for the child who made it.

2) Model of a Temple

Supplies:

> Milk cartons, washed and taped shut
> Plain white paper
> White Contac™ paper (optional)
> Glue
> Scissors
> Construction paper
> Tape

Some advance preparation needed.

Each child will need a clean milk carton to build a temple. The temples in this case will look like a traditional church with a steeple.

Tape the open end of the carton up so that it is a rectangular block. Cover the carton, either with the Contac™ paper, or by gluing white paper around the sides.

Begin by having the children roll a piece of construction paper into a cone for the steeple. Tape the seam. Make four half inch long cuts around the bottom of the cone, so that flaps can be folded out. Glue the steeple to the milk carton church by these flaps. Make sure and hold it on for awhile so that the glue sticks.

Next let the children decorate the churches. They can use markers, or glue windows and doors on. Suggest stained glass windows and big double doors.

As the children work, talk about how Jesus's church, or temple, would have been different than the one they are making.

Baptism

Talking Together

If you haven't had an opportunity to attend a baptism as a class, take the children to the sanctuary and let them see the baptismal font close up. Talk about baptism in your church. Tell them you will be telling a story about Jesus' baptism (Matthew 3; Mark 1:1-11; Luke 3:1-22; John 1:19-34) but it will be very different than their own baptisms.

Introduce John the Baptist as Jesus' cousin. Talk about his ministry of baptism, washing away wrongs and welcoming people to a life with God.

Then tell about Jesus' baptism in the river, and of the dove and the voice of God. Explain that this is the beginning of Christ's ministry.

Art Projects

1) Doves

Supplies:

> Heavy white paper
> Scissors
> Tape
> Hole punch
> Yarn
> Black and yellow markers

Some advance preparation needed.

Before class cut bird bodies and wings out of white paper. If your class is adept with scissors, you could simply draw patterns on the paper and let them do the cutting.

Have the children cut a slit in the bird body, as wide as the wings. Insert the wings through the body, and secure with tape. Then add black eyes and a yellow beak with the markers.

Punch a hole in the top of the bird and string yarn for hanging the bird. Hang them all together from the classroom ceiling for awhile, then let the children take them home.

2) Pine Cone Bird Feeders

Supplies:

> Pine cones, the big stiff kind
> Peanut butter
> Bird seed
> Plastic bags
> Paint shirts
> String

Gathering supplies is the only preparation needed.

Make sure to have the children wear paint shirts because this is a messy project.

Have the children pack peanut butter into the pine cone. There should be enough to fill its nooks and crannies, but not so much that you can't see the cone any more. Then have them roll the cone in bird seed. The seed will stick to the peanut butter and make an attractive treat for birds.

Tie a piece of string around the cone for the children to hang the feeders. Either hang them all in a tree by the church, or send them home in plastic bags.

3) Dove Flags

Supplies:

> Either colored felt or construction paper
> Thin dowels or long plastic straws
> Scissors
> Glue

Some preparation is needed.

Before class cut doves out of white felt or white paper. If your class is good with scissors they may be able to cut from a pattern, but remember that cutting felt can be tricky.

Let each child choose a color for his or her flag and cut a square big enough to accommodate the dove. Even younger children will be able to cut a rough square with help.

Glue the doves to the squares, then glue the flag to a dowel or straw. Make sure to hold it to the dowel for a while so that it sticks. Stapling the flag to a wooden dowel works as well.

The flags can illustrate the story of the baptism in two ways. First of all, the dove is like the one that appears in the story. Secondly, the events in the story act as a sign to the people around Jesus, pointing him out as the Messiah. The flags are also signs.

Gathering The Apostles

Talking Together

The apostles were Jesus' special friends. Tell the children that as Jesus travelled around teaching, many people followed him and helped him. Twelve were his closest friends who were always with him. Tell them the stories of how Jesus chose these men. (Matthew 4:18-22, 9:9, 10:1-4, 19:16-24; Mark 1:16-20, 2:13-14, 3:13-19, 10:17-25; Luke 5:1-11, 27-28, 6:12-16, 18:18-25)

Talk to the children about what the apostles had to leave behind when they decided to follow Jesus. Explain that in trying to live as Jesus taught us we may have to give up things we want. As examples describe a friend who wants them to steal some candy, and choosing between keeping all the money they earn for themselves or giving some to help others.

Art Projects

1) 3D Fish

Supplies:

Stiff paper, tag board or poster board

Multi-colored tissue paper

Scissors

Glue

Some advance preparation needed.

Cut the tissue paper into 1 inch squares. Make sure you have a variety of colors. Cut a fish shape out of the stiff paper, about 7 inches long. If the children are older you may just draw a fish pattern and let them cut it out themselves.

Have the child smear a thin layer of glue onto a section of the fish, about 3 inches square. Put a finger in the middle of a tissue paper square, and wrap the sides up around the finger. Then press the finger, with the tissue paper still on it, onto the glue. Take the finger out, leaving a little cup made from tissue paper. Do this with more tissue squares, placing them close together to fill the fish. Smear more glue in small areas as needed.

2) Fishing Game
Supplies:
>Stiff paper or thin cardboard
>Large paper clips
>Thin wooden dowels or long thin sticks
>String
>Tape
>Markers

Some advance preparation needed.

Before class cut fish shapes out of the stiff paper, about three inches long. Make three or four for each child.

Give each child a dowel for a fishing rod. Help them tie a piece of string to the end, about 18 inches long. Secure the string with a piece of tape wrapped around the pole. At the end of the string tie a paper clip, then bend the clip into a hook.

Let the children color their fish in with markers. When they are decorated slip a paper clip onto the front, with at least half of it sticking out from the paper. Secure the clip with tape. The children can try to hook the fish by the paper clip.

If you want, fancier magnets can be used instead of paper clips. This does make it easier for the children to catch the fish. Get the tiny round magnets that are used for refrigerator magnets. Glue one to each fish. A paper clip hook still works, because the metal attracts the magnet.

3) Nets Full of People
Supplies:
>Stiff paper or thin cardboard
>Markers
>Construction paper

One of the following nets:

A. Mesh bags from oranges
B. Small plastic bags and permanent black marker
C. Large envelopes
D. White paper cups

Some preparation is needed.

Before class cut people shapes out of the stiff paper. Make men and women similar to those used on the doors at public restrooms; these are familiar symbols to children. They should be at least three inches tall, so that children are able to decorate them.

In class let the children decorate some people. They can either color them with markers, or cut clothes out of construction paper and glue them on. If you can get some patterned paper, either old wrapping paper or wallpaper samples, these can make good clothes as well.

There are several alternatives for making the nets to put these people into. Which method is chosen depends on the skills of the children and the availability of supplies.

A. Mesh bags such as those oranges are sold in are probably the most attractive and the easiest nets to use. However, they are not always available. A separate bag for each child is best, since they have a bag to put the people in. If there are not enough bags, they could be cut into smaller nets. Make sure they are big enough to fit several people.

B. Clear plastic bags can also make an easy net. Help the children draw criss-crossed lines on the bags with a permanent black marker. The people can be slipped into the bag. (Caution: please remember that plastic bags can present a danger to children.)

C. Large envelopes can be used for nets as well. They are not as attractive as other alternatives, but easily made. Fold the envelopes in half and in half again. Along each side cut out two or three squares. Leave strips of the envelope intact along each edge and between the squares. Unfold envelope.

D. White paper cups are the most basic nets. Have the children draw criss-crossed lines around the cup to represent the net. Place the people inside the cup.

Curing the Sick

Talking Together

There are several stories about Jesus curing the sick. (Matthew 8:1-4, 8:14-15, 9:1-8; Mark 1:23—2:12; Luke 4:33-41, 5:17-26) Group the stories together to talk about this part of Jesus's ministry. The stories are repetitive, so there is no need to go into the details of each one. Choose one of the stories and tell it more fully, while only mentioning the others.

Small children listen to a lot of fairy stories and will quickly start relating Jesus' miracles to "magic." To direct them away from this, explain that as the Son of God Jesus was a special teacher. God wanted people to listen closely to what Jesus told them, so Jesus was given abilities that most people do not have. Jesus used his strength to help other people. And Jesus wants us to help other people.

While telling the healing stories try to find ways to help the children understand the afflictions Jesus healed. Talk about how a blind person uses touch. Put a familiar object inside a pillow case and have a child try to identify it by touching. Have an object for each child. Talk about paralysis. Have a child stand in front of you, hug her tightly around her arms and ask her to move. Then suddenly release her and let her arms fly up. Spend some time mouthing words without a voice to demonstrate deafness. When the children tell you to talk, act like you don't understand them.

A good way to illustrate the "helping message" of the curing stories is to have a doctor come visit the class. If you have a doctor in your church who would be good with small children ask her to come and speak about healing people. Explain that a doctor cannot heal with a touch like Jesus could, but that she is using her special abilities to help people get well. Ask the doctor to bring in some of the tools she uses in treating patients and share them with the children. A stethoscope, ear scope, and x-ray are good examples.

Talk about other ways that the children can help other people, even if they are not sick.

1) The Helper Sticker Chart

Supplies:

Paper

Rulers

Markers

A selection of stickers

Gathering supplies is the only preparation needed.

The children will be making charts to take home and keep track of times they help someone else. After they collect a specified number of stickers they bring the chart back to class to get their "Helper Awards."

At the top of each piece of paper write "Jesus Helped People; So Do I." At the bottom of the paper show the children how to use the ruler to draw a row of boxes. Decide how many stickers they will need to put onto the chart in order to get their award; that's how many boxes they need. In the space between the boxes and the writing the children can draw a picture of helping. This could be a picture of Jesus healing a sick person, or of them helping dry the dishes.

Attach enough stickers to fill in the boxes. Either send written instructions home with the chart, or talk to parents about it. If you are worried that some children will just put the stickers on the charts themselves, ask parents to make a small note about what they did to earn the stickers. Then you can talk about it with them and praise their efforts.

When the full chart is returned to you, have some kind of an award planned. Pencils, small pins, or more stickers are easily bought. To make an award either cut a ribbon out of construction paper and pin it to the child's shirt, or write up a fancy looking award certificate. If the church has a computer, try printing award certificates.

2) Helper Medicine

Supplies:

Clean empty jars

Circles cut out of construction paper

Dark pen

Labels for the jars

Some preparation needed.

Make sure there is a clean jar for each child. They need to be big enough to hold a collection of the paper "pills." Cut circles out of construction paper, small enough to fit in the jar, but big enough to write several words on.

Sit with the children and have them suggest things they can do to help around the house. As they talk write tasks on the circles and drop them into their jars. Make sure the tasks are within their real abilities. Suggest ideas like "Help pick up" or "Give Mom a big hug."

Labels for the jars can be purchased mailing labels, or glue on labels made from paper. Write "Helper Medicine" on each label, then let the children decorate them.

Tell the children that their parents will be able to take a "Helper Pill" whenever they need help at home. When the children help, they will be following Jesus.

3) Get Well Cards

Supplies:

> Paper
>
> Markers or crayons
>
> Collection of decorations, glitter, sequins, magazine pictures
>
> Glue
>
> Scissors

No advance preparation needed.

Show the children how to fold the paper to make cards. Talk to them about the kind of cheerful pictures that will help a sick person feel better. Then let them get to work on the front of the cards.

If some of the students are able to write or copy letters, let them write "Get Well" inside the cards. If not, write it for them. Many four- and five-year-olds can write their own name, so have them sign the cards.

There are three ways to send the cards. Let the children take them home and use them there. Send them to people in the church who are sick or shut in at the time you make the cards. Or keep them on hand in the room with a stack of envelopes and whenever you hear of someone who is sick, let the children send a card. Don't wait for catastrophic illness; send them out for colds and sprained ankles, too.

4) Musical Get Well Card
Supplies:

Tape and tape recorder

Gathering supplies is the only preparation needed.

Have the children record songs on a tape to give to a sick member of the church or a shut in. Begin the tape with each child saying his or her name. Then sing a song or two and end with a big good-bye. Let the children listen to themselves, but make sure they know it will be passed on to someone who needs cheering up.

Blessing the Children

Talking Together
The story of Jesus calling the children to him (Luke 18:15-18) is a favorite of children. It gives them an image of Jesus they can relate to and find comfort in. Relate it to events in their own lives. All children have had the experience of being hushed or made to feel unwelcome. Let them see that Jesus felt children were valued in the eyes of God.

Art Projects
1) Child of God T-shirts
Supplies:

A plain t-shirt for each child

Fabric paint in two or three colors

Waxed paper

Newspapers

Gathering supplies is the only preparation needed.

Children's t-shirts bought in packages are not terribly expensive, but if the cost is too much for the Church School, ask each parent to donate a shirt.

Do this project on the floor, with newspapers under the t-shirts. Also fold a sheet of newspaper to fit into the shirt and keep the paint from soaking through to the back.

Work with one or two children at a time. They will need supervision to make sure they don't get paint everywhere. Make sure they wear paint shirts.

Put a little fabric paint on a piece of waxed paper. Let the children smear it around with their hands. It washes off easily afterwards. Then have the child put his hand prints on the shirt. Let him decide how many prints to make and where to put them. If he wants to do multiple prints, make sure he gets more paint on his hands.

After the hand prints are on the shirt, an adult should use fabric paint to write the child's name and "Child of God."

Leave the shirts to dry until the following week.

2) Photo Posters
Supplies:
> Pictures of the children
> Construction paper
> Glue
> Scissors
> Markers

Take photos of the children in advance, unless there is an instant camera available.

Each child will make a poster about herself. In the center attach the photo of the child. It will look more finished if you make a mat around it. First glue a square of black paper that is slightly larger than the photo to the poster, and attach the photo on top of that.

Underneath the photo have an adult write "God Made Me Special Because" then help the child list three or four special things about herself.

Finally let the children decorate the rest of the poster. Encourage them to draw things that represent their lives, a picture of their house or church, of their family or pets.

3) Plaster Hands or Hand prints

Supplies:

> Plaster of Paris Mix
> Bowl for mixing
> Pitcher of water
> Disposable pie tins

or   Large construction paper
> Paint
> Waxed paper

Gathering supplies is the only preparation needed.

For Plaster Hand Prints: Mix plaster and water according to the directions on the plaster mix. Make a fairly thick paste. Pour it into the pie tins, smoothing the surface for a nicer appearance. Bend a paper clip into a loop and stick it into the plaster, positioning it at the top, between the pie tin and the plaster. This will serve as a hanger when it is dry.

Have the children put their hand into the plaster. Tell them not to put it in so deep that they touch the pie tin, but make sure they are really in the plaster. They will need to hold their hands still for a short while, until it starts to set. Plaster hardens quickly. Let the plaster dry for a week before you try to remove it from the tins.

For Paint Hand prints: Write "God Made Only One {Child's Name}" at the top of each piece of paper. Put a little paint on the waxed paper and let the children smear it around. Help them to press their hand firmly onto the paper. Make sure they don't smear it around.

4) A Jesus and the Children Mural

Supplies:

> Large bulletin board paper
> Markers or crayons
> Smaller pieces of paper

or   Photos of the children in class, and magazine pictures of children

Advance preparation needed.

This project requires some artistic ability from an adult. A picture of Jesus should be drawn on the bulletin board paper before class. Traditionally he is seated with outstretched hands in pictures with the children, but this is not necessary. He should be holding his hands out to bless the children.

There are two ways to add the children to this mural. Using markers or crayons have the children draw pictures of each other. Assign each child to draw a portrait of a friend. Talk about using hair color, glasses, color of skin, and clothes as ways to identify the children.

Or create a collage of pictures of children around the Christ figure. Let the children cut photos of children from magazines. Then add photographs of the students in your class.

Feeding the Five Thousand

Talking Together
The miracle of the loaves and fishes (Matthew 14: 13-21; Mark 6:35-44; Luke 9:12-17; John 6:1-14) illustrates Jesus's concern for the people who followed him, and their earthly needs. It also raises the subject of Jesus's increasing power because of the number of followers he had. This can be valuable to touch on, since it foreshadows the events of Easter.

Art Projects
1) Popcorn Party:
Supplies:
> Popcorn and a popcorn popper
> Juice
> Bowls and cups for serving
> Party decorations, balloons, streamers, etc.

Some advance preparation needed.

The week before the party will occur invite some guests. Parents or pen pals are good, or another Church School class.

Let the children decorate the room for the party. When the guests arrive have them sit down with the children. Explain that the class has been talking about the miracle of the loaves and fishes. Now the children have a great number of people to feed at their party, but they can't perform a miracle. The popcorn is a symbol for the bread, because it starts out small, but ends up able to feed many. Then pop the popcorn together and have a good time.

2) 5,000 People Collage
Supplies:
>Collection of old magazines
>Big piece of stiff paper
>Scissors
>Glue

Gathering supplies is the only preparation needed.

Make a collage of faces to represent the 5000 that Jesus fed. Have the children cut out as many faces as they can and glue them to the stiff paper. Try to find magazines with many different kinds of people represented.

3) Bread Banks
Supplies:
>Empty, clean milk cartons
>Brown paint and paint brushes
>Clean, empty bread bags and twist ties

Gathering supplies is the only preparation needed.

These are good banks for the children to collect coins for a special offering. Dedicate the money to a food shelf or UNICEF or another organization that supplies food for the hungry. Set a date that the children will return their banks to the Church School. Make sure to let parents know what the bank is for and when it should be brought back.

Tape the top of the milk cartons shut and cut a slit in the top for the coins. Have the children paint them brown, to look like bread. The cartons won't hold paint all that well, but since they will be in a bread bag it will be all right. Let the paint dry.

Slip each bank into a bread bag and tie it shut. Cut a slit in the bag to match the one in the bank. Glue the bag to the bank around the slit, but otherwise let it remain loose like a real bread loaf.

Chapter Eight

Lent And Easter

Talking Together

Talking with preschoolers about Lent and Easter is a delicate job. The story of power, betrayal, and the crucifixion is painful. It is not the sort of story one would generally choose for three-year-olds. It is, however, the core of the Christian faith.

It is possible to avoid the story of the Passion of Christ by dealing with Easter in a general way, by talking about rebirth after winter, spring flowers, and animals. This is a more secular view of Easter, however.

Before the Easter season arrives decide how the story will be told. It can be broken into parts and told over the course of a few weeks. Begin with the entry into Jerusalem, then tell about the last supper and the betrayal. Recount the death and the resurrection in the same day, rather than leave them with the vision of the crucifixion for a week.

For younger or more sensitive children soften the impact by being direct, but leaving out details. Older children will be more able to listen to a full recounting of the events. Be prepared for blunt questions such as "How did they get Jesus to stay on the cross?" Deciding in advance which details to leave out will not always work since children invariably ask for more.

If you are concerned about a child's reaction talk to his parents. Invite them to sit in on class during the story telling.

And remember that the Resurrection is the heart of Easter.

Art Projects

1) Cross Necklaces
Supplies:
> Paper clips
> Selection of beads, about the size of peas

Yarn or string

Needle nose pliers (optional)

Some preparation needed. (Remember that small beads may present a danger to young children. The children should be closely supervised.)

The paper clips will be used to make wire crosses on which beads can be strung. Five-year-olds may be able to unfold the wire and twist the crosses. For younger children make the crosses in advance. A needle nose pliers helps with the bending.

To make the wire crosses straighten two paper clips. Wrap one around the other to make the cross shape. It will slip up and down, but the beads will hold it in place. Have the children put two or three beads on each branch of the cross. Bend the wire at the end of each branch over to secure the beads. At the top bend the wire into a loop.

String some yarn through the wire loop and tie it around the child's neck as a necklace. More beads can be strung on the yarn.

2) Popsicle Stick Crosses

Supplies:

Popsicle sticks

Glue

Clay (as described on page 34)

Gathering supplies is the only preparation needed.

Make the crosses by gluing two popsicle sticks together. The children may trim them with markers, or by gluing decorations on them. While the glue dries make the clay to use as stands for the crosses. Give each child a ball of clay about the size of a small orange, have them press it to the table so that it stands flat, then stick the cross into it.

3) Planting Seeds

Supplies:

Paper cups

Large seeds or beans

Potting soil

Gathering supplies is the only preparation needed. Remember that seeds or beans may present a danger to young children. The children should be closely supervised.)

Fill each cup with potting soil. Help the child bury the seed in the dirt and water it. If there is someone on the church staff who will keep the dirt moist during the week, leave it in the classroom until they sprout. This allows you to watch them with the class and talk about how seeds are symbols of rebirth.

4) The Rising Sun

Supplies

> Construction paper, black, yellow, dark blue, light blue, orange
>
> Scissors
>
> Glue
>
> Stapler

Some preparation needed.

A lot of cutting is needed for this project. If the children are younger, cut the pieces out in advance and let them do the gluing. If the children are adept with scissors, simply draw guidelines on the papers in advance.

The end product will be a five page book showing the rising of the sun.

Page one is simply a black piece of paper.

Page two is a black piece of paper with a 1/2 inch wide strip of orange paper glued across the bottom.

Page three is a dark blue piece of paper with a 1/2 inch strip of orange glued across the bottom. Directly above the orange a curve of yellow is glued to the middle of the page, representing the first curve of the sun. If a really dark blue shade of construction paper isn't available, use purple.

Page four is a light blue piece of paper. The 1/2 inch strip of orange remains the same. A half circle of yellow is glued to the middle, directly above the orange. Across the top of the paper glue a strip of dark blue paper, two inches wide.

Page five is a light blue piece of paper with a full circle of yellow in the middle, with thin strips of yellow around it for the rays of the sun.

Staple the book together across the top edge.

5) Color Easter Eggs

Supplies:

> Boiled or blown eggs
>
> Easter egg dye kit

Some preparation needed.

Hard boil or blow the eggs before class. To blow an egg make holes in each end with a sharp pin. Then blow into one end, forcing the contents out the other and into a bowl. If it is difficult to force the egg out, enlarge the holes slightly. Rinse with a gentle stream of water. Although this makes an egg that can be kept much longer than a boiled egg, they are quite fragile.

Dye the eggs according to the instructions on the coloring kit. While coloring the eggs talk about why they are Easter symbols.

6) Empty Tombs

Supplies:

> Clay (as described on page 34)
>
> Paint and brushes
>
> Squares of cardboard
>
> Large paper cups, cut in half
>
> Tape

Some preparation is needed.

Make the clay before class, since the children will need time to sculpt and paint their tombs.

Tape a half cup to each piece of cardboard, cut side down. This forms the cave for the tomb. Have the children cover the cup in clay. They can also use clay to make scenery around the tomb.

Give each child a piece of clay to roll into a ball, big enough to be the stone which covers the door of the tomb.

Allow the pieces to dry and then paint them.

7) Paper Palms

Supplies:

>Stack of newspapers
>
>Tape
>
>Scissors
>
>Green spray paint (optional)

Gathering supplies is the only preparation needed.

Unfold a sheet of newspaper and lay it flat. Begin to roll it into a tube from one side. Halfway place another sheet of newspaper on top of it, and continue rolling so that the two sheets make a tube together. Tape the edges.

From the top cut slits half way down the length of the tube. Make four slits, one on each side. Holding the center of the paper at the top, carefully begin to pull up. The papers will telescope out to form "leaves."

To make the palms green, take them outside and spray with a light coat of spray paint.

8) Have a Parade

Supplies:

>Palm branches, real or made as above
>
>Stiff paper, tag board or poster board
>
>Newspapers
>
>Tape
>
>Horns and kazoos (optional)
>
>Tape of marching music (optional)

Some preparation needed.

Get permission to march a parade either through the other classrooms, or through the adult services.

Have the children make signs with Easter symbols on them, or proclaiming "Jesus Lives" or "Arise!" Make the signs on the stiff paper. Tightly wrap several sheets of newspaper into a tube and tape the edges. These make good temporary sticks for the signs. Staple the stiff paper to the tubes.

March with the tape playing, or with the children making noise. Practice in the classroom a bit before taking the show on the road.

Chapter Nine

Finishing The Year

Talking Together

End the year on a positive note. Spend some time remembering things the class has done together. Talk about how much the children have grown over the past year. Encourage parents and pen pals to come to the last day of class and help celebrate the Church School. If the weather is nice, have a picnic. If that isn't possible have a party indoors with decorations and a special snack.

Projects

1) Church School Photo Albums

Supplies:

> Pictures of the children taken throughout the past year
> Construction paper
> Photo corners or double sided tape
> Stapler

Gathering supplies is the only preparation needed.

Help each child make a photo album to remember the year in Church School. Divide the photos up so that each child has a few. Show them how to attach them to a piece of paper with the photo corners or tape. Let them use markers or crayons to decorate the pages. Make sure and write the names of the children in each photo underneath the picture. Finally, put the pages together and staple.

2) Take Home the Jesus Story Books

If the children have been making Jesus Story Books, make sure to have them take them home. A few weeks before the last day of class check to make sure they are finished.

3) Class Photo and Frame

Supplies:

       Picture of the class, one copy for each child

       Stiff paper, tag board or poster board

       Glue

       Collection of decorations, glitter, sequins, stickers

       Scissors

       Markers

Advance preparation needed.

Take a photograph of the class a couple weeks before the last day so that a copy can be made for each child.

Cut two squares of the stiff paper, each about an inch bigger than the photograph. One square is for the backing, the other will be the frame. For the frame, cut out the center but leave a border of a little more than an inch all around.

Before gluing the frame together have the children decorate it. Have an adult write the church's name and the year on each one.

Tape the photo to the middle of the backing paper, then let the children glue the frame over it.

4) Graduation

Supplies:

       Diplomas

Advance preparation is needed.

Have a graduation ceremony for children who will be moving into other classrooms in the fall. Type up diplomas certifying that they have finished their Preschool Christian Education. Sign the bottom and make a gold seal out of colored paper. Roll it up and tie a ribbon around it for presentation. Make sure to invite parents and pen pals to the party.